A UNIQUE MIRACLE

Quran Stories for Little Hearts

by
SANIYASNAIN KHAN

Helping you build a family of faith

2

The Prophet Isa (Jesus) ﷺ was born in a town called Bayt Lahm (Bethlehem), five miles south west of Jerusalem. He grew up in Nasiriya (Nazareth).

4

One day his disciples asked him
whether his Lord could send down
a table spread with food from the
heavens.

'Go in fear of Allah,' warned Isa عليه السلام, 'if you are true believers.'

8

But they insisted and in answer to the Prophet Isa's prayer, angels brought down a table spread with delicious food—a special miracle quite different from all others.

The Prophet Isa عليه السلام continued his mission for several years, but only a few answered his call.

The Children of Israel,
wanted to kill him by
crucifying him on a cross.

12

13

But Allah saved him and they crucified another man who was made to appear like him.

Lo, I am the servant of Allah:
Allah has given me the Book,
and made me a Prophet.
Blessed He has made me, wherever I may be;
and He has enjoined me to pray,
and to give the alms, so long as I live,
and likewise to cherish my mother,
He has not made me arrogant, unprosperous.
Peace be upon me, the day I was born,
and the day I die,
and the day I am raised up alive!

- Surah Maryam
19:30-33

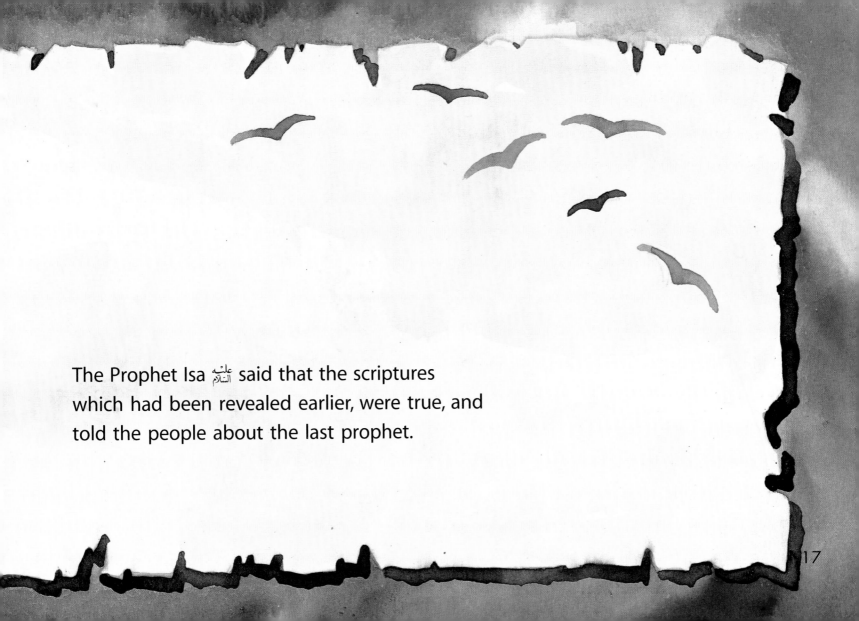

The Prophet Isa ﷺ said that the scriptures which had been revealed earlier, were true, and told the people about the last prophet.

He said, 'I am sent forth to you from Allah to confirm the Tawrat already revealed, and to give you news of a messenger who will come after me whose name is Ahmad.'

The Prophet Isa ﷺ went up to
heaven from the town of Nasiriya.

There are sayings of the Prophet Muhammad ﷺ which tell of the return of the Prophet Isa عليه السلام to the earth before the Day of Judgement.

Find Out More

To know more about the message and meaning of
Allah's words, look up the following parts of the
Quran which tell the story of the Prophet Isa ﷺ.
  Surah al-Ma'idah 5:112-115